The Book of Work from Work Cartoons

Featuring Cartoons From
Barron's
The New Yorker
The Wall Street Journal
and more!

Index of Artists

Cover illustration: David Borchart
Book Design: Darren Kornblut

Cartoon Collections, LLC, 10 Grand Central, 29th Floor, New York, NY 10017

For cartoon licensing information visit www.cartoonstock.com

ISBN: 978-1-963079-02-9 / First edition published 2024

"If I put mustaches on all of us, we look more like a team."

"*Actually, I got some pretty good ideas when I was in the box.*"

"When you're nailing the numbers, they don't ask questions."

"Got your e-mail, thanks."

"Do we want to just flip a coin,
or hire expensive consultants so they can flip a coin?"

"He Replied All."

"I try to keep my coffee buzz going till the Martini buzz kicks in."

"Psst. Is everyone still mad at me?"

"So how do you like these new cylindricals?"

"I'm so glad you decided to participate in our
Money for Employment program."

"Nope, no New Year's resolutions for me this year—I'm still working on a backlog dating from '87."

"Oh, I'm all business, but I find that a talk-show format works well for me."

"We can still be friends, Roger. I just don't want you to be one of my vice-presidents anymore."

Shanahan

"This is my stop, Phil, you'll be C.E.O. till Sixty-third Street."

CASUAL PAYDAY

Shanahan

BONFIRE OF THE PAPERWORK

"Now that you've met all the people who could easily replace you,
I'd like you to meet the person who is actually going to replace you."

"You need to get out here — we just had another texting-while-walking mishap."

"Okay then, that's four 'yays' and one 'neigh'..."

"My greatest asset is my ability to tell you exactly what you want to hear."

"Actually, we all think you're doing a pretty good job. We just feel it would be more fun to have a celebrity for C.E.O."

"Damn it, Chalmers, can't that wait until at least July?"

"In five years, I see myself with the same job title, about the same salary, and significantly more responsibilities."

"Sir, I have a question that's lunch-related."

"I'm going to bombard you with graphs until you agree with me."

"I've just never worked anyplace where
the 'alpha male' was a woman."

"I'm really glad I don't work on this floor."

"Don't flash the wrong gang sign or they won't hold the elevator."

"It keeps people from falling asleep during meetings."

"We can't offer you a golden parachute, however we do offer a very attractive escape hatch."

"*This is highly confidential, so, yes, we built a little fort.*"

"Not only did we get the account we snagged 'Best in Show' too."

"Okay, I'll renew your contract and raise you five sick days."

"But this is the way we've always done it."

"*Any questions?*"

"Just an FYI before we go up to the meeting, Filkens, the one who ran all the Zooms, her head is way smaller than you're expecting."

"*I know you're one of my friends, but I'm replacing you with a follower.*"

"I don't dress for work till I'm actually working."

"*Change in plans - the deadline's been moved up to four days ago.*"

"Hey, it's good to finally put a face to the obnoxious emails."

"If it's all the same to you chief, I'd like to work from home tomorrow."

www.ingramcontent.com/pod-product-compliance
Lightning Source LLC
Chambersburg PA
CBHW040848100426

42813CB00015B/2745

The Book of Work from Home Cartoons

Featuring Cartoons From
Barron's
The New Yorker
The Wall Street Journal
and more!

Index of Artists

Cover illustration: Teresa Burns Parkhurst
Book Design: Darren Kornblut

Cartoon Collections, LLC, 10 Grand Central, 29th Floor, New York, NY 10017

For cartoon licensing information visit www.cartoonstock.com

ISBN: 978-1-963079-02-9 / SKU: 46495
First edition published 2024

"I thought we agreed you weren't going to work at home."

P. BYRNES.

"Off to work, Hon. See you tonight."

"Look at you! Breaking out the good sweatpants today."

EVOLUTION OF ZOOM

Week 1

Week 2

Week 3

Week 4

"I can't tell if she needs to stop goofing off or take a break from studying."

"*Remember, as soon as his boss joins the video conference, it's showtime.*"

"It just seems to me, Howard, that you're missing the
whole point of having a terrace in the city."

"I can't remember – do I work at home or do I live at work?"

"I'd love to meet up, but my calendar is a jam-packed
with squares and sequential numbers."

"Can't we just do this online?"

"So working from home is no longer an option?"

"You really think they'll come back to the hill after they've gotten used to working remotely?"

"Who's coming with me?"

WORKING FROM HOME 2.0

"Working at home has been a mixed blessing."

"*Most of all, I enjoy being able to work at home.*"

"Honey, can you close the door? I'm in a meeting."

"Oh, are you attacking from home today?"

"Let's take an excruciatingly awkward two minutes for people to trickle in."

"O.K., in three... two... one..."

"It's the only room I'm not totally bored of."

"Later on, after work, do you want to have leftovers."

"See? And you said you couldn't work from home."

"You're right–this is way better than a standing desk."

"*Your ten o'clock cancelled. He doesn't like the way his skin gets all wrinkly.*"

"Sorry I'm late. I tripped over
a laundry basket on my way to my computer."

"I didn't get the job. They hated my Zoom background."

"I wouldn't mind being a stay-at-home dad
if I didn't have stay-at-home kids."

"I take it you're video conferencing all day from home?"

"There's no place like work... There's no place like work..."

"If you won't let me work from home, then
I'll just home from work."

"I prefer to work from home."

"It's just me today. Everyone else is working remotely."

"....and Brian, down there, is just here
to even out our grid."

"*Your meeting's over. You can relax you zoom face now.*"

"Sure, it looks clean, but believe me, right out of camera view it's a mess!"

"Just because they all work from home now doesn't
mean I don't still keep an eye on them."

"We were hoping that you could work from work today."